GRIMALKIN

GRIMALKIN
and other poems

Thomas Lynch

[signature]

For John.
well met in
Fayetteville
write on
good stories.
TL
'95

CAPE POETRY

First published 1994

1 3 5 7 9 10 8 6 4 2

© Thomas Lynch 1994

Thomas Lynch has asserted his right
under the Copyright, Designs and Patents Act, 1988
to be identified as the author of this work

First published in the United Kingdom in 1994 by
Jonathan Cape
Random House, 20 Vauxhall Bridge Road, London SW1V 2SA

Random House Australia (Pty) Limited
20 Alfred Street, Milsons Point, Sydney,
New South Wales 2061, Australia

Random House New Zealand Limited
18 Poland Road, Glenfield,
Auckland 10, New Zealand

Random House South Africa (Pty) Limited
PO Box 337, Bergvlei, South Africa

Random House UK Limited Reg. No. 954009

A CIP catalogue record for this book
is available from the British Library

ISBN 0 224 03973 3

Typeset in Bembo by
SX Composing Ltd, Rayleigh, Essex
Printed and bound in Great Britain
by Mackays of Chatham PLC

THIS BOOK IS FOR MARY TATA

A nod should be given to customs that disappeared. Puckle tells of a curious functionary, a sort of male scapegoat called the 'sin-eater'. It was believed in some places that by eating a loaf of bread and drinking a bowl of beer over a corpse, and by accepting a six-pence, a man was able to take unto himself the sins of the deceased, whose ghost thereafter would no longer wander.

Habenstein & Lamers
The History of American Funeral Directing

Love is like a stove. It burns you when its hot. Love hurts.

words & music by Boudleaux Bryant
as sung by Roy Orbison

ACKNOWLEDGEMENTS

Some poems in this work were originally published in the following publications, to whose editors the author expresses his thanks:

Adrift, Agni Review, Ann Arbor Magazine, Boston Review, Chouteau Review, Colorado-North Review, Cyphers, The Great Lakes Review, Hiram Poetry Review, Honest Ulsterman, Mid American Review, Midwest Quarterly, MSS, Paris Review, Poetry, Poetry Ireland Review, The Quarterly, River Styx, Salmon, Southern Review, Southwest Review, Virginia Quarterly Review, Visions International, Witness.

Some of the poems collected here were also published in *Skating with Heather Grace* (Knopf, 1986).

The author wishes to make known his permanent indebtedness to Michael Heffernan, John F. Nims and Gordon Lish.

'Rhododenrons' was published in broadside by Bernard Stone of the Turret Bookshop, London.

Special thanks to Donald Sheehan of the Frost Place and Bernard and Mary Loughlin of the Tyrone Guthrie Centre for the Arts in Newbliss, Co. Monaghan.

The completion of this book was assisted by fellowship grants from the National Endowment for the Arts and the Michigan Council for the Arts.

CONTENTS

Certain of these poems take, for their titles, the names of Gregorian hymns in Latin. These plain chants were common to the Roman Catholic liturgies until the early 1960s when the Second Vatican Council englished everything. When I was a child, Latin was the language of faith and adoration. It was strange, magical, sacred and dead. To those who sense the meaning of those hymns, maybe even sing along, I recommend *Chants of the Church*, edited and compiled by the Monks of Solemes, published in 1953 by the Gregorian Institute, from which the following interlinear translations are taken:

Attende Domine et miserere: Attend O Lord, and have mercy
Pange lingua: Sing (my) tongue
Inviolata, integra, et casta: Inviolate, untouched, chaste
Parce Domine mei: Spare me Lord
Veni, Creator Spiritus: Come Creator Spirit
Panis Angelicus: Bread of Angles
O Gloriosa Virginum: O (thou) glorious among virgins
Adoro te devote latens deitas: I adore thee devoutly hidden deity
In Paradisum deducant te: Into paradise be thou conducted

Moveen is a townland on the west coast of Ireland, in Clare, on the peninsula that forms the upper lip of the mouth of the River Shannon. It is where my people come from and where my cousin, Nora Lynch died at almost ninety in 1992. Her brother, Tommy Lynch, died in the spring of 1971. Both are buried in the graveyard at Moyarta, just south of Moveen, near the estuarial village of Carrigaholt. I first visited these places in February of 1970 and have returned many times since.

Mercywood is the name of the sanitarium in Ann Arbor, Michigan, to which Roethke was taken for treatment of manic-depression. The treatment of choice then was hydrotherapy. Certain lines in the ninth section of 'Learning Gravity' are Roethke's, including 'Love begets love' and 'I watch the river wind itself away' from 'The Motion' in *The Far Field*. From the same poem, 'Knowing how all things alter in the seed' became, in mine, 'Who knows how all things alter in the seed?'

TL

ATTENDE DOMINE

To lie in the tub on New Year's morning
awash in bath oil and resolution,
observing the Feast of the Circumcision,
is to seek the water's absolution
according to the law that juxtaposes
Cleanliness and Godliness. I suppose
it is time to examine my conscience,
to make a clean breast of it and amends
to such as those I might have offended.
Attende Domine et miserere! Lord
I've sinned with my eye and did not pluck it out,
and with my hand and yet my hand remains
blessing myself against Your righteousness.
I've sinned with my mouth and loved the sound it made.

LIBERTY

Some nights I go out and piss on the front lawn
as a form of freedom – liberty from
porcelain and plumbing and the Great Beyond
beyond the toilet and the sewage works.
Here is the statement I am trying to make:
to say I am from a fierce bloodline of men
who made their water in the old way, under stars
that overarched the North Atlantic where
the river Shannon empties into sea.
The ex-wife used to say, Why can't you pee
in concert with the most of humankind
who do their business tidily indoors?
It was gentility or envy, I suppose,
because I could do it anywhere, and do
whenever I begin to feel encumbered.
Still, there is nothing, here in the suburbs,
as dense as the darkness in West Clare
nor any equivalent to the night-long wind
that rattles in the hedgerow of whitethorn there
on the east side of the cottage yard in Moveen.
It was market day in Kilrush, years ago:
my great-great-grandfather bargained with tinkers
who claimed it was whitethorn that Christ's crown
        was made from.
So he gave them two and six and brought them home –
mere saplings then – as a gift for the missus,
who planted them between the house and garden.
For years now, men have slipped out the back door
during wakes or wedding feasts or nights of song
to pay their homage to the holy trees
and, looking up into that vast firmament,
consider liberty in that last townland where
they have no crowns, no crappers and no ex-wives.

THE SIN-EATER

Argyle the sin-eater came the day after –
a narrow hungry man whose laughter
and the wicked upturn of his one eyebrow
put the local folks in mind of trouble.
But still they sent for him and sat him down
amid their whispering contempts to make
his table near the dead man's middle,
and brought him soda bread and bowls of beer
and candles which he lit against the reek
that rose off that impenitent cadaver
though bound in skins and soaked in rosewater.
Argyle eased the warm loaf right and left
and downed swift gulps of beer and venial sin
then lit into the bread now leavened with
the corpse's cardinal mischiefs; then he said
'Six pence, I'm sorry.' And the widow paid him.
Argyle took his leave then, down the land
between hay-reeks and Shorthorns with their calves
considering the innocence in all
Gods manifold Creation but for Man;
and how he'd perish but for sin and mourning.
Two parishes between here and the ocean.
A bellyful tonight is what he thought,
please God, and breakfast in the morning.

THAT SCREAM IF YOU EVER HEAR IT

You know who you are you
itchy trigger fingered sonovabitch
always at my elbow with your
'Rub their noses in it.
Give it to them raw.
Spare the cutesy metaphor and bullshit.
Say what it was you heard or saw without
one extra syllable.'

How some biker with a buzz-on
doing eighty in a forty-five
broadsides a Buick
killing the babies buckled in the front seat
leaving the babies' mother with a limp,
a lengthy facial scar,
a scream stuck in her somewhere
north of her belly, south of her teeth.

I know you don't need symmetry or order
so that the biker died in pieces –
the arm with the tattoo reading SHIT
HAPPENS thrown a hundred yards from the one
with NO TOMORROW on it – doesn't impress you.
But here's a little truth
you will approve my telling of:
The mom is going to leave her husband
fight with her father,
curse the priest.

She is going to go and live in the city,
have her face fixed, drink too much,
begin to sleep around in search
of the one and only one who can
tickle that scream out of her.

Maybe you'll run into her.
Maybe you're the one.

Here's another thing you will appreciate.
I know you'll like this. Listen up:
That scream, if you ever hear it,
won't rhyme with anything.

WHERE IT CAME FROM

Where it came from if it came from anywhere
was the deep pit within him where his anger was
hunched like a bad beast back on its haunches
ready to hunker up whenever he got ready
whenever he'd had enough of this or when
love turned sour left him out of love.

Trouble was whenever he got troubled
by something lesser men got lessened by
or needled by some needless hurt or
thought of some lost intimate he only thought
Good God! Might all this come to some last good
to ease the ache I've grown lately accustomed to?

Furthermore he seemed to draw no further
comfort from those things he once drew comfort
from: Ease of wit and easy motion from
one good hideout to another. Once
when he was at his peak of loneliness he went
nowhere for a good long while where he wasn't known.

PANGE LINGUA

This is the voice I talk to myself in.
The one that says, before I fall asleep,
the children will all grow up and outlive me;
my mother's tumour will be benign;
the women who loved me will always love me.
This is the same voice I heard as a child
the time I first ate meat on a Friday,
at Bobby Bacon's house. It said, Baloney.
Or when I lingered over magazines
Jim Shryock and I found stashed in his basement –
conscience and complicity: the voice that sings
Pange Lingua in the shower nowadays,
sings the glorious body's mystery
of blood and bliss and love and misery.

A FAMILY OF FISHERMEN

In all his dreams of death it was his heart that failed him.
It ran in the family like bellies and tempers
and though his mother's people favoured the long pull
and died mostly of kidneys or pneumonias,
skinny and bewildered in their nineties, all
the men drank whisky and died of big hearts,
huffing and puffing to their purple ends.
So he held to his history and was ever ready
for one bolt out of nowhere that would lay him low
with only the juice left for one last wisdom,
maybe: *I always loved you* or *I told you so*
or *I must be dreaming*. He must have dreamt
a hundred times of how his great-great-grandfather
after a half day's fishing the cliffs at Doonlickey
could feed the whole parish on pollack and mackerel
till one day somehow he turned up missing
and washed up later in the bay at Goleen
wrapped up in his tackle of ribbons and sinkers
and made, in spite of it, a lovely summer corpse.
So he lit out in the pitch dark with the same instincts,
crossing the winter of his lake to where
he banged at the bare ice till his heart was breaking,
because of beauty, because the cold stars seemed
the blank eyes of women he had always loved,
and he told them so and thought he must be dreaming
to see his family, a family of fishermen,
approaching as the day broke under snowfall, so
he lay down in the first few inches of it.

VIGIL

Rose, you are the winter-oak
whose spent leaves redden and remain
limp emblems of the heart's accustomed hold
on this – the known life of seasons,
daylights, nightfalls, weathers –
the ordinary calendars, mean time.
Ordinarily we live our lives out
hopeful and afloat among the rounded metaphors:
seedtime and harvest, dark and dawn;
solstice and equinox, calm, storm.
Ignoring the linear paradigms we move
buoyantly between our pasts and futures
gamely trading prospects for remembrances,
deaf to the regular changing of tenses –
those doorways slamming down the narrowing hall.
Behind the doors, we hear the voices still:
Goodnight. Godspeed. God Bless. Get Well. Goodbye.
The deaths we seldom grieve but set our watches by.

SKATING WITH HEATHER GRACE

Apart from the apparent values,
there are lessons in the circular:
paradigms for history,
time in a round world, turning,
love with another of your species –

To watch my only daughter
widening her circles is to ease
headlong into the traffic
of her upbringing.

Until nearly four she screamed
at my absence, mourned
my going out for any reason,
cried at scoldings,
agreed to common lies regarding
thunder, Christmas,
baby teeth. Last year

she started school
without incident;
this year ballet and new math. Soon

I think my love will seem
entirely deficient.

Later there's the hokey-pokey
and dim lights for the partners' dance.
She finds a shaky nine-year-old
to skate around
in counter-clockwise orbits,
laughing.

Is it more willingness than balance?
Is letting go the thing that keeps her steady?

I lean against the side-boards sipping
coffee. I keep a smile ready.

CUSTODY

Every other weekend they go to their mother's.
Some Tuesdays or Wednesdays they spend the night.
She takes them for two weeks in the summer.
We divvy up the holidays. Otherwise
they live here, with me. We agreed to this
after months of court-appointed enmity
during most of which we behaved like children.
In the end, I was 'awarded custody' –
a legalese to make it sound like winning –
pancakes and carpools and the dead of nights
with nightmares or earaches or wet bedlinen.
Their mother got what's called her visitation rights –
a kind of catch-up-ball she plays with gifts
and fast-food dinners-out and talk of trips
to Disneyworld in the sparkling future.
They were ten, nine, six, and four when it happened.
I played their ages in the Lotto for awhile.
I never won. They were, of course, the prize.
They were, likewise, the ones, when we were through
with all that hateful paperwork and ballyhoo,
who seemed like prisoners of care and keeping
and settled into their perplexed routines
like criminals or parties to a grief –
accomplices in love and sundering.

ARGYLE IN VAPOURS

Vaporous and sore at heart, Argyle stood
in his doorway looking out at nothing.
The wind blew through him as if he wasn't.
As if he were, himself, a door ajar
through which one had to go to get nowhere
and wanting to go nowhere, there he stood –
a spectacle of shortfall and desire.
And all the voice of reason in him reasoned was
'Take heart, Argyle! This is seasonal.
The winter is a cruel but equal cross
borne only by the living in the name of Christ,
and though a cold encumbrance on the soul afire
with ministry and purpose, bear in mind
the dead will keep for days in such weather
and any climate so kind to a corpse
will shorten purgatory for those left alive
to huddle in their mud and wattles for some warmth.'
Such comfort as that gave him helped him weather
well enough the chill and shortened days,
the noise of rats wintering in his thatch,
the endless bitter merriment at wakes.
By dark he dreamed the touch of female flesh –
all night in sweats and brimming scenes of pleasure
and waking up alone, he blamed the weather.

TO HER SISTERS ON THE NATURE OF
THE UNIVERSE

I think of all landscapes as feminine
and of the many seasons as a man
whose weather is the ever-changing reason
he will give for wanting you. As for hands,
I think of them as daybreak and nightfall
hourly easing over my skin. My skin
is the morning you awaken to snowfall
drifting to berms and swells and shallowings
like tidal oceans overtaking land.
I think of oceans as the way a man
returns to me from exile or wars,
blood-drunk and frightened to the bone. Of course
he hears her then, asleep between my breasts –
the angel charged with beckoning the dead;
and wakes up gladsome for the soft iambic code
my pulse assures him with: Not yet, not yet.

MAURA

She had never desired him in that way —
that aching in the skin she'd sometimes get
for a man possessed of that animal something.

Something outside of language or regret. No,
he'd been the regular husband, the hedged bet
against the baglady and spinsterhood;

a cap on the toothpaste, the mowed lawn, bills paid;
a well-insured warm body in the bed,
the kindly touch if seldom kindling.

Odd then, to have a grief so passionate
it woke her damp from dreams astraddle him —
the phantom embraced in pillows and blankets,

or sniffed among old shirts and bureau drawers.
She fairly swooned sometimes remembering
the curl of her name in his dull tenor.

Sweet nothings now rewhispered in her ears.
She chose black lace, black satin, reckoning
such pain a kind of romance in reverse.

The house filled with flowers. She ate nothing.
Giddy and sleepless, she longed for him alone.
Alone at last, she felt a girl again.

INVIOLATA

I had a nunnish upbringing. I served
six-twenty Mass on weekdays for a priest
who taught me the *Confetior* and to keep
a running tally of the things I'd done
against the little voice in me the nuns
were always saying I should listen to.
And listen is what I did and spoke the truth
of it to Father Kenney in confession,
and walked out with a clean slate, listening,
listening. At thirteen what it said was Tits.
Tits everywhere. Even Sister Jean Thérèse –
Inviolata, integra et casta –
for all her blue habits and scapular,
standing at the blackboard, sideways, couldn't hide
    them.

A DEATH

In the end you want the clean dimensions of it mentioned;
to know the thing adverbially – *while asleep,*
after long illness, tragically in a blaze –

as you would the word of any local weather:
where it gathered, when it got here, how it kept
the traffic at a standstill, slowed the pace,

closed the terminals. Lineage & Issue, Names & Dates –
the facts you gain most confidence in facing –
histories and habitats and whereabouts.

Speak of it, if you speak of it at all, in parts.
The C.V.A. or insufficiency or growth
that grew indifferent to prayer and medication.

Better a tidy science for a heart that stops
than the round and witless horror of someone who
one dry night in perfect humour ceases measurably to be.

GRIMALKIN

One of these days she will lie there and be dead.
I'll take her out back in a garbage bag
and bury her among my son's canaries,
the ill-fated turtles, a pair of angelfish:
the tragic and mannerly household pests
that had the better sense to take their leaves
before their welcomes or my patience had worn thin.
For twelve long years I've suffered this damned cat
while Mike, my darling middle-son, himself
twelve years this coming May, has grown into
the tender if quick-tempered manchild
his breeding blessed and cursed him to become.
And only his affection keeps this cat alive
though more than once I've threatened violence –
the brick and burlap in the river recompense
for mounds of furballs littering the house,
choking the vacuum cleaner, or what's worse:
shit in the closets, piss in the planters, mice
that winter indoors safely as she sleeps
curled about a table-leg, vigilant
as any knick-knack in a partial coma.
But Mike, of course, is blind to all of it –
the grey angora breed of arrogance,
the sluttish roar, the way she disappears for days
sex-desperate once or twice a year,
urgently ripping her way out the screen door
to have her way with anything that moves
while Mike sits up with tuna fish and worry,
crying into the darkness 'here kitty kitty',
mindless of her whorish treacheries;
or of her crimes against upholsteries –
the sofas, love seats, wingbacks, easychairs
she's puked and mauled into dilapidation.

I have this reoccurring dream of driving her
deep into the desert east of town
and dumping her out there with a few days feed
and water. In the dream, she's always found
by kindly tribespeople who eat her kind
on certain holy days as a form of penance.
God knows, I don't know what he sees in her.
Sometimes he holds her like a child in his arms
rubbing her underside until she sounds
like one of those battery powered vibrators
folks claim to use for the ache in their shoulders.
And under Mike's protection she will fix her
indolent green-eyed gaze on me as if
to say: Whaddaya gonna do about it, Slick,
the child loves me and you love the child.
Truth told, I really ought to have her fixed
in the old way with an air-tight alibi,
a bag of ready-mix and no eyewitnesses.
But one of these days she will lie there and be dead.
And choking back loud hallelujahs, I'll pretend
a brief bereavement for my Michael's sake,
letting him think as he often said
'deep down inside you really love her don't you Dad.'
I'll even hold some cheerful obsequies
careful to observe God's never-failing care
for even these, the least of His creatures,
making some mention of cat-heaven where
cat-ashes to ashes, cat-dust to dust
and the Lord gives and the Lord has taken away.
Thus claiming my innocence to the end,
I'll turn Mike homeward from that wicked little grave
and if he asks, we'll get another one because
all boys need practice in the arts of love
and all boys' ageing fathers in the arts of rage.

LATE APRIL

Six months to the morning since the day you died.
Another heartsore Friday full of sun,
temps in the sixties, a stirring in the trees.
We have put a winter in between our griefs –
between the gaping hole and greening sod,
between the wet funeral and dry one.

There was a comfort in the numbers then.
We counted priests and limousines, flowers,
favours, the sympathies and casseroles
of those who came and followed to the end
in keeping with the common sense that holds
a strength in numbers: the more the merrier.

Late April now and now the number One
assumes its upright stance – the walking wound
that pauses among monuments to count
another season's emblements of loss:
one grave, one stone, one name on it, one rose,
one fist to shake in the face of God then go.

THERE THERE

He wanted to be a victim of something,
to get on a talk-show and spill his guts
on just how it was he came to be this way –
the awful dysfunction of his upbringing
the sorry particulars of which he could make up
to fit the prime-time appetite for pain.
Just once he wanted the studio audience
to moan in disbelief on his behalf
and for Oprah to take his hand in her hand
and tell him There There Everything Will Be Alright.

ARGYLE IN AGONY

Some sins Argyle couldn't stomach much.
Sins against virgin girls and animals,
women bearing children, men gone blind
from all but self-abusive reasons gave him
stomach troubles, like over-seasoned meat
he oughtn't to have eaten, but he always did.
Some nights those evils woke him in his sleep –
gaseous and flatulent, bent over his puke bowl,
resolved again to draw the line somewhere,
to leave the dirty work to younger men
or anyway, to up his prices.
Maybe steady work with nuns whose vices
were rumoured to go down like tapioca.
But no, those clever ladies lived forever
and for all their charities would starve the man
who counted for his feed on their transgressions.
Better to go on as he always had,
eating sins and giving souls their blessed rest.
What matter that his innards heaved against
a steady diet of iniquities
or that children worked their mayhem on his head
by carving pumpkins up in fearful effigies?
He had his holy orders and his mission.
He had the extreme unction of his daily bread.

THESE THINGS HAPPEN IN THE LIVES
OF WOMEN

The first time he ever bought her lingerie
she was dead of gin and librium and years
of trying to regain her innocence.
'These things happen in the lives of women . . .'
is what the priest told him. 'They lose their way.'
And lost is what she looked like lying there
awash in her own puke and the disarray
of old snapshots and pill bottles,
bedclothes and letters and mementoes of
the ones with whom she had been intimate.
She was cold already. Her lips were blue.
So he bought her a casket and red roses
and bought silk panties and a camisole
and garters and nylons and a dressing gown
with appliqués in the shape of flowers.
And after the burial he bought a stone
with her name and dates on it and wept aloud
and went home after that and kept weeping.

RHODODENDRONS

It was the dream
I was allowed
to touch you in.
We were strangers.
You kept your eyes closed.
I cannot really say
if there were rhododendrons
or anything like music or
even if I asked you.
Only your blue skin
and the pleasure it gave you –
the way you moved,
the way you caught your breath
whenever my hands moved
so I kept on moving them.

PARCE DOMINE

Maybe I oughtn't to be naming names.
Maybe Sister Jean Thérèse is still alive,
married to a former priest or nine to five
with one of those human service agencies.
Maybe Bobby Bacon lives on fruits and cheese
or joined some eastern cult of vegetables.
Maybe Jimmy Shryock works the vice patrol
or has a TV ministry. Who knows?
I know Father Kenney retired to Salthill
and died of eighty years. As for the rest,
maybe I should have used an alias.
Maybe what I should have said was 'breasts'
though tits is what they seemed and ever shall seem
world without end. *Parce Domine Mei.*

LIKE MY FATHER WAKING EARLY

Even for an undertaker, it was odd.
My father always listened through the dark,
half-dreaming hours to a radio
that only played police and fire tunes.
Mornings, he was all the news of break-ins, hold-ups,
now and then a house gone up in flames
or a class of disorder he'd call, frowning,
a *Domestic*. They were dying in our sleep.
My father would sit with his coffee and disasters,
smoking his Luckies, reading the obits.
'I've buried boys who played with matches
or swam alone or chased balls into streets
or ate the candy that a stranger gave them . . .'
or so he told us as a form of caution.
When I grew older, the boys he buried toyed
with guns or drugs or drink or drove too fast
or ran with the wrong crowd headlong into peril.
One poor client hung himself from a basement rafter –
heartsick, as my father told it, for a girl.
By sixteen, I assisted with the bodies,
preparing them for burial in ways
that kept my dread of what had happened to them busy
with arteries and veins and chemistries –
a safe and scientific cousin, once removed
from the horror of movements they never made.
Nowadays I bury children on my own.
Last week two six-year-olds went through the ice
and bobbed up downstream where the river bends
through gravel and shallows too fast to freeze.
We have crib deaths and cancers, suicides,
deaths in fires, deaths in cars run into trees,
and now I understand my father better.

I've seen the size of graves the sexton digs
to bury futures in, to bury children.
Upstairs, my children thrive inside their sleep.
Downstairs, I'm tuning in the radio.
I do this like my father, waking early,
I have my coffee, cigarettes and worry.

NO PRISONERS

Odds are the poor man was trying to please her
because her pleasure would have pleasured him
adding as it would have to his image of
himself as a latter-day Man of Steel,
able as always to leap tall buildings
and off of whose chest the bullets would bounce,
his five bypasses notwithstanding,
nor withstanding how his heart had grown
flimsy with hard loving and bereavement.
Or maybe it was the Marine Lance-Corporal
in the snapshot of himself in the South Pacific
he kept in the corner of the bathroom mirror:
bare-chested in khakis and boondockers
with Billy Swinford Smith from Paris, Kentucky,
posing as always for the girls back home;
the ready and willing eighteen-year-old
who went from right tackle with St Francis DeSalles
to light machine-gunner with the Corps
and came home skinny and malarial later
to marry the red-headed girl of his dreams
who had written him daily through the war,
beginning her letters with *My Darling Edward*
and closing with *All My Love Always, Rose.*
We found those letters, years later, in a drawer
and tried to imagine them both young again,
dancing to Dorcey and Glenn Miller tunes
under the stars at the Walled Lake Pavilion
before they had any idea of us.
'Six sons,' he'd laugh, 'enough for Pallbearers!
and girls enough to keep us in old age.'

So when our mother took to her bed with cancer,
it was, of course, the girls who tended her
while my brothers and I sat with him downstairs
being brave for each other. When she died
he knelt by her bedside sobbing 'Rosie,
My Darling, what will I do without you?'
And grieved his grief like Joe DiMaggio
who never missed a game and took a rose
to place in the vase at her graveside daily
then came home to sit in his chair and weep.
Those first nights without her thereby replacing
as the worst in his life a night in '44
on Walt's Ridge in Cape Gloucester, New Britain
when he and elements of the First Marines
survived nine Bonzai charges. The Japanese
foot-soldiers kept screaming, kept coming, blind
into the crossfire of light machine guns
that he and Billy and Donald Crescent Coe
kept up all night aiming just below the voices.
In the morning he crawled out of his hole
to poke his bayonet among the dead
for any signs of life and souvenirs.
Whatever he found, he took no prisoners
and always said he wondered after that
how many men he'd killed, how he'd survived.
He'd try to make some sense of all of it
but if he did, he never told us what it was.
And now he is dying of heartache and desire.
Six months into his mourning he became
an object of pursuit among the single set
of widows and divorcees hereabouts;
the hero of a joke his cronies tell
that always ends with *But what a way to go!*

Last night mistaking breathlessness for afterglow,
a woman nearly finished him with love
and barely made it to the hospital
where they thumped his chest and ordered oxygen.
The First Marines are off to war again.
He watches CNN in ICU
while leathernecks dig trenches in the sand.
The president says No More Vietnams.
The doctors tell him Easy Does It, Ed –
Six weeks, six months, who knows. It's up to you.
Avoid excitement, stimulation, sex
with any but familiar partners.
He tells them War is Hell. It takes no prisoners.
A man must have something worth dying for.
The Persian skies are bright with bombs and fire.
My father's sleep is watched by monitors
that beep and blink – his sore heart beating, still.
I wonder if he dreams of soldiers killed
in action – Japanese, Iraqis, old Marines
who died for flags and causes but in the end,
among their souvenirs, we only find
old snapshots of their wives and women-friends.

ARGYLE'S EJACULATIONS

Argyle's preference in sins was legend.
The best of them were those the priests invented:
broken fasts or abstinence in Lent,
a tithe unpaid or Sunday morning passed
in honest, gainful labour or in bed.
He feasted full on Easter Duties missed
or some bad-mouthing of a Jesuit.
He relished churchy sins that had no flesh
or blood or bones, but only upset
some curate's dictum on moral etiquette.
'God Bless His Holiness in Rome O Lord!' –
Argyle often ejaculated –
'And all Right Reverend Eminence & Graces,
and all the idle time they have to kill
concocting new sins for my evening meal.'
But then he'd dream that girl-child again,
defiled by some mannish violence who threw
herself to death, despairing, down a bog hole.
And when the parish house refused her requiems
her people sent for Argyle to come
and undo by his dinner what the girl had done.
But Argyle knelt and wept and refused the bread
and poured the bowl of bitters on the ground
and prayed, 'God spare my hunger till that
    churchman's dead.'

LEARNING GRAVITY

Here is how it happens. One soft night
you're sitting in an outdoor bar with friends,
glad for the long days and your own survival,
which has come for the time being to depend
upon what conversation you can make
out of Beethoven or the cinema,
out of the way the loss of light proceeds
from top to bottom in the sky, always
abiding by those few sure-footed laws
whereby things rise and fall, arrive and take
their leave according to their gravity –
earthbound, in balance, timely and at ease.
When who shows up among the tabletops
but somebody you haven't seen in years.
You follow him into another room
and find him staring in a wall of mirrors.
He doesn't know how long it's been or what
he's done. He has no plans, he says, except
to be gone tomorrow. Much later, on
account of this, you will begin to grieve.

That time in Moveen, the sky became
so full of motion the soft air seemed
too quick a thing to breathe in, so I sang

out where the gulls glide on the edge of weather
songs in praise of rootlessness and wayfare
and wore my newfound whereabouts with honour

the way a man does who goes travelling
without a war on or a famine:
c/o third cousins, West Clare, Ireland.

My Love, I wrote home in a letter, here
the old arrangement of the rock & water
gathers up the coastline in a lather.

The slate cliffs lean with the weight of land
into the heft & heave of ocean.
I watch the tide fall and rise and fall again.

I thought of you then as a secret in the water
that made waves out of the elements of order
and taught them surge and swell and billow

so the air filled with a rich noise below
the tall ledge of land I edged along
dizzy with the sweet enticement of the fall.

Kennedy had been dead by then for years.
My fall from innocence
began with a still frame from Zapruder's film –
a blurry likeness of the way he leaned
into his wife's hug with the look of damage,
and how she cuddled him as if he were
a bingy drunk who only liquored up
for holidays or funerals or for fun.
I thought, how much she loves him,
how surely dead he seems. Since then
I measure my departure from where I was
that day, in Christian Brothers' School
and the flat voice on the p.a. saying
all that we could do was pray.
I put you with the nuns, next door, that day –
your life in those times parallel with mine,
arranged by height or alphabet for sacraments.
First Communion, Confirmation,
the Death of Presidents.

I remember my poor cousin in his bed.
A quiet replica of calm,
his mouth propped shut with his daily missal.
A rosary kept his hands crossed on his chest.
Inside the women hummed their beads and sipped
sweet wine and ripe Cidona. In the yard
the men complained of prices and the spring that left
a mudwreck of their fields and kept their cows in.
'The Lord've mercy on him, Tommy was
a daycent man he was and innocent.
A pure St Francis with his cattle, shy
when it came to women or the drink.
Sure Faith, there was no speck of sin in him.'
And then in deference to his Yankee namesake,
bloodshot from the porter or the grief,
they brought their hopeless talk around to Kennedy.

His was the first death in our lives that took.
Until then our heroes were invincible:
the cartoon cat who swallows dynamite,
the cowpoke who turns up in a rodeo
after getting murdered in a barfight.
That was the apple we bit for truth:
the permanence of death for him, for us
the death of permanence. For days
we watched him go the way of the
Friday Meat Rule and the Latin Mass,
the rhythm method, black and white TV,
true love and romance, our favourite saints,
Cardinal Sins, Contrary Virtues, all
parts of life we'd made a part of us that changed.
O Jack, here thirty years since then,
we think of you as lovable and dead.

Your pink notes came up the coast road with the
    postman.
Word about friends, weddings and the spring

in Michigan, and Roethke, whose growth of poems
you'd grown enamoured of. 'He sings and sings

root tunes and seed songs, hums the fern and foliage.'
Of course, he'd learned the lesson in his garden –

how one day getting on to Autumn
you come across hard knowledge like a corpse

left out in the dull light by some passion,
murderous or accidental, nonetheless

passion of a human sort. You appraise the body's beauty:
a leptosome among the leaves. The rare lines

of the ribs poke out beneath the skin
like kite-work of some former elegance. The leaves rise on

the small ground wind. The birdlike beauty lies
solid in its lack of movement, quiet as the moon is,

drinking the darkness like the moon does, turning
damp and fertile. Going to seed.

With this intelligence you begin, then,
thick with excitement and new fright.

I remember the bones of my kinsmen,
long since dead, unearthed again in the grave's
reopening – femurs and half-skulls and ribs
in piles at graveside at Moyarta.
And the general reverence of townsmen,
neighbours, thick countrymen from the creamery
or local bog, thatchers and fishermen,
all of whom had doings with our newly dead.
All of whom had come to their consensus
after Mass, in boozy In Memoriams:
'An honest airy man he was. By cripes,
the saint of the peninsula! A far,
far better specimen than the likes of us.'
When the priest said so, we made for Moyarta,
shouldering the saint of that peninsula
into the hilly middle ground between
the River Shannon's mouth and the North Atlantic.

Consider Roethke in his tub at Mercywood,
crazy with his glad mayhem, how he would
soak for hours like a length of bogwood

lolling and bobbing in the water.
I think of you, your body in the water
and how the light glistened in the beads of water

that ran down between your breasts like islands
among the bare geographies I learned
the year that we were lovers, after Ireland.

Who knows how all things alter in the seed?
From shoot to stem to full bloom then to seed,
clumsy with their own invention until they see

that everything that breathes requires death.
A fierce affection is a thing like death.
Love begets love, then life, then death.

I watch the river wind itself away,
delighted at your bright flesh drying, at the way
the earthly body learns its earthly ways.

1948 – Expect from birth
68.6 years, give or take.
A useful figure for, say, figuring
career options, life goals, middle age,
with further applications in the abstract:
to arrive at what to expect from death, subtract
the Useful Figure from Infinity.
The Crude Death Rate for 1963 was
nine point four per thousand, which includes
infant mortality, less the foetal deaths,
a poet, Roethke, and a President.
1970 – some notable variants:
bad flu in the Middle West,
the same war in Asia, always
pestilence in the usual places.
The remarkable number: 100%.

I'm the one who keeps a rough count of the dead.
I count whatever's unclaimed after months
of reasonable inquiries, want ads, word of mouth –
things get around once word gets out.
It's a small place we live in, after all.
Which explains the recent interest in your case.
Because it seems you've come into your strength
by learning gravity and pause and keeping pace
so that you fall no faster than thirty-two
feet per second per second and you move
always in accordance with the rules of life
that govern bodies moving in the realm of light.
What is it you keep faith in, hope for,
count your blessings by? Life after death?
Death after life? After sex a cigarette?
Why is it I have come to think of you without
a history or vision or the dreadful tow
of things that moved us and the way we went
out into the real world full of innocence,
passion, and mortality? I don't know.
But things happen every day here.
We could all be alive tomorrow.

Sometimes I come here for a drink with friends.
Sometimes I drink too much and feel like crying
God, God! I'm a sad man with a thin heart dying
from complications of a complex race of men
who all their lives look for holes to fill
with all their lives. Their lives and loss of will.

VENI CREATOR SPIRITUS

And spare me Lord, likewise, my memory of
a woman's body rising from the bath –
the diamond water shining on her back
and how she turned towards me, the way that Eve
most surely turned towards Adam in her flesh
before embarrassment or baptism or death,
before love meant a willingness to die
or gibbet of the cross, before the wine
got consecrated into blood – Good Christ –
before the fall, the flood and days of wrath,
before the latter sacraments of death.
Veni, Creator Spiritus, create
once more the body's easy mystery:
the water, water; the wine, wine; the bread, bread only.

WEST HIGHLAND

Whenever I hear their aged names –
Lena, Cora Mae, Lydia, Bea –
I think of prim, widowed ladies from
the Baptist Church in West Highland Township;
and imagine their ordered, born-again lives
beyond the latter-day suburban sprawl
of disenchantment and convenience stores.
Lives lived out at the same pace as their mothers
and their mothers' people years before them,
between pot-lucks and bake sales and bazaars,
missions and revivals, Sunday to Sunday.
And for romance, they had 'Nights to Remember' –
in summer, the Bible School picnics,
October, the Farm Bureau Harvest Ball.
All winter long, they courted in parlours
with men named Thurmond or Wilbur or Russell Lloyd.
They married at Easter and bore children
and outlived their husbands and tend the graves now
after Sunday services, weather permitting.
Whenever I see them, arm in arm,
at funerals where they sing or bring baked hams
in memory of one of their sisters, dead
of the long years or the nursing home,
I think of how the century for them
was neither wars nor science nor the evening news
but a blur of careful rites of passage:
baptisms and marriages and burials.
And I envy their heavens furnished like parlours
with crocheted doilies on the davenport
and Aunt Cecelia, who never got married,
singing 'In The Garden' or 'Abide With Me'
and God the Father nodding in His armchair
at saints and angels who come and go
with faces like neighbours and with names they know.

FOR THE EX-WIFE ON THE OCCASION
OF HER BIRTHDAY

Let me say outright that I bear you no
unusual malice anymore. Nor
do I wish for you tumours or loose stools,
blood in your urine, oozings from any orifice.
The list is endless of those ills I do not pray befall you:
night sweats, occasional itching, PMS,
fits, starts, ticks, boils, bad vibes, vaginal odours,
emotional upheavals or hormonal disorders;
green discharges, lumps, growths, nor tell-tale signs of
    grey;
dry heaves, hiccups, heartbreaks, fallen ovaries
nor cramps – before, during, or after. I pray you only
laughter in the face of your mortality
and freedom from the ravages of middle age:
bummers, boredom, cellulite, toxic shock and pregnancies;
migraines, glandular problems, the growth of facial hair,
sagging breasts, bladder infections, menopausal rage,
flatulence or overdoses, hot flashes or constant nausea,
uterine collapse or loss of life or limb or faith
in the face of what might seem considerable debilities.
Think of your life not as half-spent but as half-full
of possibilities. The Arts maybe, or
Music, Modern Dance, or Hard Rock Videos.
Whatever, this is to say I hereby recant
all former bitterness and proffer only all the best
in the way of Happy Birthday wishes.
I no longer want your mother committed,
your friends banished, your donkey lovers taken out and
    shot
or spayed or dragged behind some Chevrolet of doom.

I pray you find that space or room or whatever it is
you and your shrink have always claimed you'd need
to spread your wings and realise your insuperable
    potential.
Godspeed is what I say, and good credentials:
what with your background in fashions and aerobics,
you'd make a fairly bouncy brain surgeon
or well-dressed astronaut or disc jockey.
The children and I will be watching with interest
and wouldn't mind a note from time to time
to say you've overcome all obstacles this time;
overcome your own half-hearted upbringing,
a skimpy wardrobe, your lowly self-esteem,
the oppression of women and dismal horoscopes;
overcome an overly dependent personality,
stretch marks, self-doubt, a bad appendix scar,
the best years of your life misspent on wifing and
    mothering.
So let us know exactly how you are once
you have triumphed, after all. Poised and ready
on the brink of, shall we say, your middle years,
send word when you have gained by the luck of the draw,
the kindness of strangers, or by dint of will itself
if not great fame then self-sufficiency.
Really, now that I've my hard-won riddance of you
signed and sealed and cooling on the books against
your banks and creditors; now that I no
longer need endure your whining discontent,
your daylong, nightlong carping over lost youth,
bum luck, spilt milk, what you might have been,
or pining not so quietly for a new life in
New York with new men; now that I have been
more or less officially relieved of
all those hapless duties husbanding
a woman of your disenchantments came to be,

I bid you No Deposits, No Returns,
but otherwise a very Happy Birthday.
And while this mayn't sound exactly like good will
in some important ways it could be worse.
The ancients in my family had a way with words
and overzealous habits of revenge
whereby the likes of you were turned to birds
and made to nest among the mounds of dung
that rose up in the wake of cattle herds
grazing their way across those bygone parishes
where all that ever came with age was wisdom.

GREEN BANANAS

My father quit buying
green bananas
for what he said were the
obvious reasons.
And made no plans – the seasons
giving way to days or parts of days
spent waiting for the deadly embolus
the doctors always talked about
to lodge
itself sideways
in some important spot
between his last breath and the one
that would not be coming after that.
Then he said Let's
go out for Chinese.
He had won-ton soup, eggrolls,
sweet and sour,
grinned when he opened the fortune
cookie. Winked at the waitress.
Left her a huge tip.
Was dead inside a month.

THE MID-LIFE OF BILL CHILDERS

By forty he had chest pains and teenagers
and every other symptom.
He had a bald spot and bad teeth and a strife
in his innards.
Anyone he had held dear
was dead by now or grown distant or moved away
or, like his children, deaf to his affections.
Women were forever wary of his attentions,
detecting in his heart of hearts
an old dog with a history of beatings.
So he sat in the same chair every night
in the darkness, watching.
He thought of Duffy in 'A Painful Case.'
He thought of Poldy Bloom. He'd seen
some women naked and observed
the terrible beauty of the universe
reflected in the way their bodies curled.
As for the dead, he only buried them.
As for the dying, he tried to keep alive
the fiction that the stars outlive
their light in some sweet firmament with God.
The rest remained a mystery to him.

PANIS ANGELICUS

Sister Jean Thérèse sold pagan babies.
At five dollars a copy I bought four,
and named them after saints and archangels
and waited for their letters. I suppose
if I haven't heard by now I never will.
Still, who is to know? Stranger things have happened.
Maybe they'll be on the next boat over.
The idea was to save their bodies
and then to claim their souls for Jesus Christ.
The old *Panis Angelicus* bowl of rice
routine. The loaves and fishes sleight of hand
that feeds the hungry, clothes the bare naked,
relieves them of their dear idolatries –
their fierce gods everywhere, gods in everything.

THE LIVES OF WOMEN

A water bucket in the birthing room
to drown the female babies in is how
they do it in the outer provinces.
In other places amniocenteses gives
fair warning to the swift abortionist.
They take the tiny foetuses away
in baskets to a retort in the basement.
The smoke their bodies burning makes is hardly
    noticed.
In over-peopled cities, fat man-children
waddle through the streets like little emperors.
Their skinny sisters, barefoot behind them,
rummage in their litter for the leftovers.
Any survivors are taken to market
arrayed in jewels and ornamental dress –
exotic packages. The men stroll through the stalls
nodding and smiling, haggling prices.
Here in the suburbs we do it with promises
of endless protection and acts of love.
We send them to good schools and make them our
    muses.
We send them to market with their credit cards,
glad in their fashions and their mini-vans.
We marry them. We call them by our names.
We do the dishes and help with the children.
We ask their opinions. We nod and smile.
We keep the buckets and baskets hidden.

THE WEST WINDOW IN MOVEEN

From here my great-grandfather stood and looked out
over the heather and blackthorn ditches
upland to Newtown where the evening moved
among the lamplit vigils of his countrymen,
each of them busy with their beads or votives,
snug in their rentals for the time being.
There was ever a wind off the ocean;
ever the prospect of rain for the haying;
ever the landlord and priest and the Mrs,
children and Friesians. He kept praying
for a signal of Divine Intention –
a voice or a vision or a holy dream
of grand living in Jackson, Michigan,
his sons with the flattened speech of Yankees,
desk jobs and dollars and early pensions.
On the best nights he would look to the southwest
over the Shannon where the Kerry hills
grew mountainous and could only imagine
the primal lives of anchorites in stone
whose holy fever forced them ever westward
to the rock cliffs of Dingle, Skelligs, and Blaskets
half-crazed from their fasts and abstinence,
willing as the sea birds or the mackerel shoals.
Maybe it was the quiet or the dark
or dreamless sleep that sent him from the land
out of Moveen with his tin footlocker –
three weeks at sea in a cheerless steerage
with Mike and Tommy, the priest I'd be named for,
and Brigid, the Mrs, who was big that time –
fat with the makings of my grandfather.

AISLING

Whenever he left her
there was always a landscape
into which he would bring her
in her linen dress
to circle a fir tree
where black birds were nesting
in the first green field
beyond the formal gardens.
He would sit at the big desk
in the bay window
in the west room they'd given him
to do it in.
He would try to describe it –
the shape of her turning
and the tune she was humming
and the way she drew
the hem of her dress up
with her small arms rising
and falling and rising
in a kind of flight,
He would try to decide if
later, by evening,
when the light was behind her
if she really knew
how the lines of her body
sharpened by twilight
would step from her clothing
in a silhouette,

if she knew how it filled him
with grief and desire
watching the gardens
and the green go black
while birds in the fir tree
settled into silence
and the great bay window
darkened where he sat –
a dark so black
he could never, ever
let her into it.

TOMMY

He keeps trying to replicate that day
in late September on the Père Marquette
when the salmon were running. How they bet
on the first fish and the most fish and the weight
of the biggest and the best. He was nine.
His mother and father were not divorced.
The salmon went upstream to spawn and die.
There seemed an order to the universe.
He has a picture of himself that day,
holding two cohos, looking capable.
Behind him trees are turning. It is autumn.
His mother is back home with Mike and Sean
and Heather, his sister, and all the while
his father keeps coaxing him: Smile! Smile!

HOW IT'S DONE HERE

We heat graves here for winter burials
as a kind of foreplay before digging in,
to soften the frosthold on the ground before
the sexton and his backhoe do the opening.
Even the earth resists our flesh in this weather –
regards the mess a new grave makes in snow
the way a schoolgirl in her new prom dress
regards defilement. It is over, though,
almost before it's started, almost routine.
The locals mount in their brisk procession,
the cleric with a few words of release
commits the body to its dispossession,
then blesses everyone, seen and unseen,
against forgetfulness and disbelief.

O GLORIOSA VIRGINUM

Truth is, I envied those pagan babies
their plentiful deities – lords in stones
and trees, goddesses of hunt and lovemaking,
their dancing liturgies in dryseason.
I envied their bodies, hungry and naked,
their bare-breasted women, unbraided hair
like the women in Jimmy Shryock's magazines
with the look of knowledge on their faces.
What I wanted was to be hungry and naked
with someone, anyone, Sister Jean Thérèse,
or the dark-haired girl in the front row – *O
Gloriosa Virginum!* And yet we seemed
sublime amid the stars, somehow at odds
with our own bright bodies and our bodies' gods.

CASABLANCA

It is always an airport
or a railway station
or one of those airy dockside rooms
folks wait in watching for the boats that move
on schedule between the outer islands.
I'm home from the big war
or a concert tour.
The news is full of my vast heroics.
One of my entourage has gone for the limo.
Another is waiting at the baggage claim.
I'm considering titles for the movie version.
And there you are, there you are, again.
Having finished your work here you have come to book
your passage on the next departure.
You are more beautiful than ever.
All of the men who loved you are dead or vanished.
I am the last man on the face of the century.

A NOTE ON THE RAPTURE TO HIS TRUE LOVE

A blue bowl on the table in the dining room
fills with sunlight. From a sunlit room
I watch my neighbour's sugar maple turn
to shades of gold. It's late September. Soon . . .
Soon as I'm able I intend to turn
to gold myself. Somewhere I've read that soon
they'll have a formula for prime numbers
and once they do, the world's supposed to end
the way my neighbour always said it would –
in fire. I'll bet we'll all be given numbers
divisible by One and by themselves
and told to stand in line the way you would
for prime cuts at the butcher's. In the end,
maybe it's every man for himself.
Maybe it's someone hollering All Hands On
Deck! Abandon Ship! Women and Children First!
Anyway, I'd like to get my hands on
you. I'd like to kiss your eyelids and make love
as if it were our last time, or the first,
or else the one and only form of love
divisible by which I yet remain myself.
Mary, folks are disappearing one by one.
They turn to gold and vanish like the leaves
of sugar maples. But we can save ourselves.
We'll pick our own salvations, one by one,
from a blue bowl full of sunlight until none is left.

ARGYLE'S RETREAT

Great hosts of basking sharks and shoal of mackerel,
like brethren in the one Creation, swam
together in the seas around Loop Head Point,
free of those longstanding habits of predation
whereby the larger fellow eats the small.
In Kilkee church, two girls saw statues move.
Lights appeared and disappeared and reappeared
from Doonaghboy to Newtown, and the dead were seen
perched upon ditchbanks with their turnip lamps by night.
In Moveen, cattle sang, crows barked and kittens flew.
The tidal pools at Goleen filled with blood
and all the common wisdoms were undone
by signs and wonders everywhere. Argyle
wondered were they miracles or omens? –
God's handiwork or some bedevilment
called up or down on him by that avenging priest
he'd lately tangled with? Either way, *retreat*
was the word formed in him. A fortnight's rest
at Dingle, fast and prayer to purge and cleanse himself
among those holy hermits there who never
once, for all their vast privations, ever
saw or heard a thing or apprehended God
abounding in their stars or stones or seas
and, for all they had not witnessed, yet believed.

BYZANCE

He gave his wife the scent that woman wore
he'd met once in the lounge-bar of the Gresham
and later took up to the suite of rooms
that overlooked the Pro–Cathedral dome
and traded mouths and hands and wetness with
then held well into the next mid-morning.

Coffee at Bewley's, lunch at Powerscourt,
they went their separate ways then with a wave –
moments only in each other's histories.
Whenever she wears that fragrance now, he is
transformed, transported, momentarily
restored to the penthouse of the Gresham:

She sits in her bright flesh at the vanity
touching herself behind her ears, between
her breasts, under her knees. She rubs her wrists
together. Pulse points she calls them, smiling.
Someone has left them mints on the pillows,
kindled the fire, turned the bedlinens down.

CONSORTIUM

Sometimes he'd sleep with her
sideways holding her
breasts in his cupped hands
pressing himself
to the bend of her body
his knees behind her knees
his feet under her feet
and bury his face
in the curls of her dark hair
and wait for the signal
her body would give him
to come inside.

ADORO TE DEVOTE

Father Kenney taught me Latin hymns.
And, lost for words, I'd often chant Gregorian:
Adoro te devote, latens Deitas –
a second tongue, more humbly to adore them in,
those hidden deities: the bodies of women,
the bodies of men, their sufferings and passions,
the sacred mysteries of life and death
by which our sight and touch and taste are all deceived.
By hearing only safely we believe.
And so I listened and am still listening.
I've heard the prayers said over open graves
and heard the pleas of birth and lovemaking.
O God! O God! we always seem to say.
And God, God helps us, answers Wait and See.

SWALLOWS

Taking the blue barrel between her lips
she thinks of all the ones who'd ever promised her
passion or romance or companionship –
a place she could call home, or a little safety.
Safety would have been enough. But they never,
after all she'd done for them, let her stay.

After all the deceptions for their egos' sake –
the pleasures pretended, the admirations feigned,
the body she gave them time and time again –
until she learned to separate her selves
and tuck away her soul, the leftovers,
the part they never wanted anyway.

Working her tongue around the bore and muzzle,
it bulges in her mouth like something natural.
The blunt head of the bullet in its chamber
rises as she cocks the hammer back. Loaded,
ready. The smooth butt in one hand, slow motion,
she grips the milky handle by its curves.

Remembering the first time and the last
she squeezes with her thumb and swallows, fast.

THE NINES

Thus we proclaim our fond affirmatives:
*I will, I do, Amen, Here Here, Let's
eat, drink and be merry.* Marriage is
the public spectacle of private parts:
cheque-books and genitals, housewares, fainthearts,
all doubts becalmed by kissing aunts, a priest's
safe homily, those tinkling glasses
tightening those ties that truly bind
us together forever, dressed to the nines.

Darling, I reckon maybe thirty years,
given our ages and expectancies.
Barring the tragic or untimely, say,
ten thousand mornings, ten thousand evenings,
please God, ten thousand moistened nights like this,
when, mindless of these vows, our opposites,
nonetheless, attract. Thus, love's subtraction:
the timeless from the ordinary times –
nine thousand, nine hundred, ninety-nine.

MONTH'S MIND

In the dream you are dead again in Florida.
The long anticipated phone call comes.
Minced fact – He's gone – and reverent detail:
something acute and myocardial
and after a good day combing the beach
collecting sea shells for the grandchildren.
Waking, I trade panic for odd relief:
dead now a month, you cannot die again.

O CANADA

Some nights he'd watch hockey and so she'd rock
with a novel or her Valéry and go to France
where she and several guests of the gay prince
picnic and play at croquet on the chateâu grounds.
Lace and ribbons are all the fashion rage
and ladies in chiffon and high coiffures
fan their bright bosoms like birds of song.
And there are men with names like pink flowers
or instruments of sound in silk stockings
and plump satin breeches to knee length who seem fond
of dabbing their roughed lip with handkerchiefs
they keep in their coat sleeves for such occasions
while all around their wigs hum yellow honeybees,
drawn to their powders and colognes and toiletries.
And she is out among them. And her hand is kissed
by gentlemen of rank and her opinion sought
on Couperin and Molière and Poussin –
all high etiquette and courtly talk.
Out in the garden, she hears the gardener sing,
between hedgerows of juniper and yew,
O Canada, our home and native land. He moves
by evening light through his green diocese,
smelling of dung and mulch and growing things,
heartsick for that hard country of his youth.
Some nights he'd take her to his room upstairs
and speak in that far dialect she loved
of ice and earth and qualities of air –
his True North, strong and free, O Canada;
and then he'd make hardbody love to her.
Next morning she'd make omelettes and he'd thumb
the newspaper for word of Guy Lafleur
or Marcel Dionne. And she'd be pleased because
that was the style of the country he'd come from.

AT THE OPENING OF OAK GROVE
CEMETERY BRIDGE

Before this bridge we took the long way around
up First Street to Commerce, then left at Main,
taking our black processions down through town
among storefronts declaring *Dollar Days!*
Going Out of Business! Final Mark Downs!
Then pausing for the light at Liberty,
we'd make for the Southside by the Main Street bridge
past used car sales and party stores as if
the dead required one last shopping spree
to finish their unfinished business.
Then eastbound on Oakland by the jelly-works,
the landfill site and unmarked railroad tracks –
by bump and grinding motorcade we'd come
to bury our dead by the river at Oak Grove.

And it is not so much that shoppers gawked
or merchants carried on irreverently,
as many bowed their heads or paused or crossed
themselves against their own mortalities.
It's that bereavement is a cottage industry,
a private enterprise that takes in trade
long years of loving for long years of grief.
The heart cuts bargains in a marketplace
that opens afterhours when the stores are dark
and Christmases and Sundays when the hard
currencies of void and absences
nickel and dime us into nights awake
with soured appetites and shaken faith
and a numb hush fallen on the premises.

Such stillness leaves us moving room by room
rummaging through the cupboards and the closet-space
for any remembrance of our dead lovers,
numbering our losses by the noise they made
at home – in basements tinkering with tools
or in steamy bathrooms where they sang in the shower,
in kitchens where they laboured over stoves
or gossiped over coffee with the next-door neighbour,
in bedrooms where they made their tender moves;
whenever we miss that division of labour
whereby he washed, she dried; she dreams, he snores;
he does the storm windows, she does floors;
she nods in the rocker, he dozes on the couch;
he hammers a thumbnail and she says Ouch!

This bridge allows a residential route.
So now we take our dead by tidy homes
with fresh bedlinens hung in the backyards
and lanky boys in driveways shooting hoops
and gardens to turn and lawns for mowing
and young girls sunning in their bright new bodies.
First to Atlantic and down Mont-Eagle
to the marshy north bank of the Huron
where blue heron nest, rock-bass and bluegill
bed in the shallows and life goes on.
And on the other side, the granite rows
of Johnsons, Jacksons, Ruggles, Wilsons, Smiths –
the common names we have in common with
this place, this river and these winter-oaks.

And have, likewise in common, our own ends
that bristle in us when we cross this bridge –
the cancer or the cardiac arrest
or lapse of caution that will do us in.
Among these stones we find the binding thread:
old wars, old famines, whole families killed by flues,
a century and then some of our dead
this bridge restores our easy access to.
A river is a decent distance kept.
A graveyard is an old agreement made
between the living and the living who have died
that says we keep their names and dates alive.
This bridge connects our daily lives to them
and makes them, once our neighbours, neighbours once
    again.

ARGYLE'S BALANCE

Argyle kept his balance feeling himself
between two equal and opposing forces
each, at once, both fearsome and endearing.
He had dreams. In one a woman in her bright flesh
kneels in the river, bathing. Later, she
lies in the tall grass drying, reddening
her nipples with the juice of pomegranates,
offering them and her body to him.
This was his dream of youth and lovemaking,
of greensong, water, all life-giving things.
The other was a dream of himself, on his
deathbed. The children gather, dumbstruck
at his belly bulbous with flatus, fat
with the old sins of others and his own.
A priest stands ready with chrisms and forgiveness.
He always dreamt this after radishes.
These were the horizontal mysteries
from either one of which he would arise
breathless with intimacy and release,
envigoured with deliverance, alive.
The answer he figured was to keep an arm's reach
between his waking self and either dream, listing
only slightly from upright anytime
the dreams made music and he would listen.

IN PARADISUM

Sometimes I look into the eyes of corpses.
They are like mirrors broken, frozen pools,
or empty tabernacles, doors left open,
vacant and agape; like votives cooling,
motionless as stone in their cold focus.
As if they'd seen something. As if it all
came clear to them, at long last, in that last moment
of light perpetual or else the black
abyss of requiems and nothingness.
Only the dead know what the vision is,
beholding which they wholly faint away
amid their plenary indulgences.
In Paradisum, deducante we pray:
their first sight of what is or what isn't.